IMAGES
of America

STONINGTON

IMAGES
of America

STONINGTON

M. Earl Smith and J. Huguenin

ARCADIA
PUBLISHING

Published by Arcadia Publishing
Charleston, South Carolina

Printed in the United States of America

Library of Congress Control Number: 2020932383

For all general information, please contact Arcadia Publishing:
Telephone 843-853-2070
Fax 843-853-0044
E-mail sales@arcadiapublishing.com
For customer service and orders:
Toll-Free 1-888-313-2665

Visit us on the Internet at www.arcadiapublishing.com

To those times when, left alone, you have to go your own way.

CONTENTS

ACKNOWLEDGMENTS

Although a book ultimately becomes an endeavor of many souls, the art, in its truest form, requires one to draw within themselves, completely independent of the outside world, and write. That being said, it would be a horrible omission to exclude thanks to the following: Erin Vosgien, Caroline Anderson, Caitlyn Post, Kiuarna Summers, Haley Johnson, Aimee Doiron, Jeff Ruetsche, Erin Owens, Aline Matushev, Jeremy Gatton, Jim Kempert, and anyone else who was not mentioned at Arcadia Publishing and The History Press; the facilities at Chatfield College, Somerset Community College, the University of Pennsylvania, Pine Manor College, Rowan University, Harcum College, and Morehead State University; Aimee Newell, Joshua Adams, Chelsea Mitchell, Beth Moore, Kaelyn Graveline, Elizabeth Wood, and the entire Stonington Historical Society Board of Directors; and Rick Stanton, Nancy Ryan, Tom Mennillo, Donna Amenett, and everyone at the Thomas Stanton Society.

Personal thanks go to Nicholas Smith, Leah Smith, Samantha Cooke, Jasmine Raghunandan, Laura Williams McCaffrey, Renee Watson, David Yoo, Brendan Kiely, Peter Stallybrass, Melissa Jensen, Nicole Flibbert, Henrique Laurino, Cathy Maclure Terrall, John Terrall, Dustin Huguenin, Eddie Smith, Kathy Smith, Kate Sydnes, Sharon King, Nayeli Riano, Maggie Rymsza, and Gustavo Ferres. And finally, to all of the shelties involved: Che, Berry, Nova, and Clover.

INTRODUCTION

Stonington is not my hometown. Its people, places, ideas, and history do not belong to me, at least in the traditional sense of belonging that one derives from their hometown. Yet as I have spent the last 13 months shacked up with the history of a place where I am a stranger, I can see why the people of Stonington love their town so. In spite of its current state as a small seaside jewel, Stonington has its roots in the working class of this country. First settled in 1649, Stonington predates the nation—and the idea that the United States was home to anyone save for the native tribes.

This project was within my view since Postcard History: *Mystic* was written in 2016. Connecticut, it seems, is dotted with little enclaves such as this, and each and every one of them has its own special appeal. Mystic is a seaside tourist village, with warships and drawbridges and a town square that brings out the best in New England. Stonington, on the other hand, is its quiet older brother, content on watching its younger counterpart enjoy its youth. That does not mean that Stonington is retired or put out to pasture. Rather, Stonington finds its history, and the people who seek to maintain it, as a reason and a purpose to get up and write a little more each day.

Stonington's history, good and bad, *is* America: the role it played in native genocide and relocation; its hand in the infancy of Connecticut; its participation in the War of 1812; the countless Irish, Italian, Chinese, Vietnamese, Cambodian, Hmong, and especially Portuguese immigrants who have called it home and a place to work for 300 years; the history of its religious convictions, which outdate America by over 100 years; its role in education, business, manufacturing, industry, commerce, trade, hunting, fishing, farming, and environmentalism; the destruction that it has faced from New England's worst hurricanes; and countless other tales of pride, woe, and anguish have all left their mark—and their scars—on the landscape of a town that is approaching 400 years old.

Every word on these pages has been fought for, struggled with, debated, considered, erased, revised, and revisited. The Stonington Historical Society, the Thomas Stanton Society, and various individuals have ensured that each symbol on the page is written to best represent what Stonington is, and what it means, on both the macro and the micro levels. This volume has been treated as lovingly as the many pieces of history that these groups and individuals have fought tooth and nail to preserve for centuries.

I am not sure if I will ever author another title about Connecticut. Time, circumstances, and the demands of a busy world tend to change the scope of what I write and when I write it. But in spite of the long, hard road out of hell that was the composition of this book, I am fiercely proud of it, and I hope it stands as a testament for both Stonington and the people who love it.

—M. Earl (Martin) Smith

One

GO YOUR OWN WAY

TRANSPORTATION IN STONINGTON

Shown here is a map of railways that connected the greater parts of Connecticut, Massachusetts, and Rhode Island and sections of Maine, New Hampshire, Vermont, and New York in 1846. The New York & Stonington Railroad was chartered in 1832 and provided service in the area by both train and ferry. In fact, the entire line was once known as the Stonington Line. Sections of the old route, ranging from Grand Central Station in New York to Kingston, Rhode Island, are still operated by Amtrak today. (Courtesy of the Boston Public Library.)

This 1880s lithograph shows one of the worst maritime tragedies in the history of Stonington: the collision between the SS *Narragansett* and the SS *Stonington*, two paddle steamers that operated along the Stonington Line, a combined rail and river line that ran as a part of the greater New York–Providence–Boston railroad. While the *Stonington* only suffered superficial damage, the *Narragansett* sank, killing 50 people. One of the survivors was Charles Guiteau, who would gain infamy a year later after assassinating Pres. James A. Garfield. (Courtesy of the Library of Congress.)

Pictured in this 1856 lithograph is the first iteration of the steamship *Rhode Island* of the Providence and Stonington Steamship Company, the origins of which date to 1837 and ownership of which changed hands numerous times before its demise in 1896. What is known today as the Stonington Town Dock and Memorial on the western edge of Stonington Point served as the steamship's terminus. By 1896, the *Rhode Island* had seen three iterations—in 1837, 1873, and 1882, the last of which was constructed by Robert Palmer at Noank. (Courtesy of the Library of Congress.)

The steamer *Richard Peck* made most of its runs between New York and New Haven. Only later in her career did she come as far north as New London and, later, Stonington. The ship, over 300 feet long and with six boilers, was one of the fastest ferries operating in Long Island Sound. Captained for most of her life by skipper Edward Hardy, she spent some of her career under the guidance of Capt. Phillip Ollweiler, who made his Stonington home on what is now Saltwater Farm Vineyards. After serving as a floating Navy barracks during World War II, the *Richard Peck* was broken up for scrap in 1954. (Courtesy of the Stonington Historical Society.)

Of the many ferries and steamers to make the run along the New England coast, the *Larchmont* was met with one of the more tragic endings. On February 11, 1907, the ship, carrying at least 156 passengers (the exact number is unknown, as the passenger list went down with the ship), rammed head-on into the coal schooner *Harry Knowlton* in icy conditions. While the schooner managed to beach, allowing all seven of its crew to survive, the ferry was not so lucky. She sank in less than 15 minutes, and only 17 passengers survived. Today, she sits in 135 feet of water less than three miles from Watch Hill. (Courtesy of the Stonington Historical Society.)

The steamboat *City of Lawrence*, named after Lawrence, Massachusetts, is pictured here from the starboard side. The *City of Lawrence* was the very first iron-hulled vessel to cruise Long Island Sound as well as the first overnight boat. It was built in 1867 by Harlan & Hollingsworth Shipyard in Delaware and was used as a replacement for the *City of New York*, which was too large to cruise the Connecticut River. The steamboat serviced the Norwich Line, run by the New York Transportation Company, owned by the Norwich & Worcester Railroad. She sadly wrecked on the Thames River in the summer of 1907. (Courtesy of the Stonington Historical Society.)

The *Massachusetts*, a 350-foot steamship weighing 3,500 tons and boasting 200 staterooms, was built in 1877. She sailed routes for the Providence and Stonington Steamship Company (incorporated in 1875), with stops in New York, Providence, and Stonington. "The famous *Massachusetts*" (as stated in a September 1891 issue of the *Cambridge Tribune*) was one of many steamships that served a full menu, complete with a wine list featuring brands still enjoyed today, like Veuve Clicquot and Moet & Chandon, both $3.50 a quart (roughly $100 today). The Providence and Stonington Steamship Company ceased operations in 1896. (Courtesy of the Stonington Historical Society.)

A paddle wheel steamer, the ferry *Block Island* was first laid down in 1882 by the Palmer Shipyard in Norwich. It would run between Norwich and the resort islands in Narragansett Bay. The New England Navigation Company, which ran the *Block Island* and several other ships, ran steamships in Long Island Sound between New York City and Boston until 1942, when the danger of German U-boat attacks put the ferries out of daily use, although some still operated for limited tourist or island transportation. (Courtesy of the Stonington Historical Society.)

The two-pillared steam vessel *New Hampshire* was the sister ship of the *Maine* and ran routes mostly between New York and New London, although she did make some trips farther north, as seen here in Stonington. She made that trip until 1935, when she was laid up. In 1937, she was scrapped in Baltimore. She was built in 1892 by Harlan and Hollingsworth Shipyard in Wilmington, Delaware. The launch of her and her sister ship coincided with the purchase of the Stonington Line by the New Haven Railroad. (Courtesy of the Stonington Historical Society.)

Built in 1881, the giant, side-wheeled steam ferry *City of Worcester* soon gained the nickname "Belle of the Sound." She was built by Harlan and Hollingsworth Shipyard in Wilmington, Delaware. Her side wheel was iron. She was 350 feet long with a 2,500-horsepower engine and the ability to hold 750 people and 110 tons of freight. She made her first trip from New York to southeastern Connecticut in 6.52 hours. She was just the second steamer to have electric lights, and the saloons and other areas were finely decorated. (Courtesy of the Stonington Historical Society.)

Shown here in a pre-1907 postcard is the steamer *New Shoreham*, which serviced a town by the same name on Block Island. The steamer frequently passed Stonington on its route. She was laid down in East Boston in 1901 and was owned by the New England Navigation Company in 1906. On June 12 of that year, she collided with the steamer *Aries*, ripping a hole in her starboard bow. In 1915, she was owned by the Block Island, Newport, and Providence Steamboat Company. On May 4, 1918, she burned to the waterline while in dock, with two crewmembers losing their lives. She was rebuilt and remained in service until 1927. (Courtesy of the Stonington Historical Society.)

The June 17, 1889, issue of *Railroad Gazette* announced the launch of the Providence Line steamer *Connecticut*. It gives her dimensions as 357 feet long, with a 6,000-horsepower engine that could push the huge paddle wheel over 30 revolutions per minute. She was 60 feet tall, painted white, and the machinery that powered her weighed over 1,000 pounds. In 1891, her schedule had her leaving Providence from dock 29 at 6:00 p.m. every day. In 1902, it was noted that she was larger than both the *Massachusetts* and the *Rhode Island*. (Courtesy of the Stonington Historical Society.)

A 3281 Steamboat Landing, Stonington, Conn.

This turn-of-the-20th-century postcard shows the steamboat landing at Stonington. On January 6, 1866, a new landing was dedicated, one that was bigger and could handle the increase in passengers and the larger steamboats that now traveled through Stonington. The larger terminus was built by John Gallup. The occasion was so joyous that the dedication featured a salute from Stonington's cannons. There was also a coalition at the Steamboat Hotel to mark this feat, which celebrated the expansion of Stonington during a period of unrivaled growth. (Collection of M. Earl Smith.)

The *St. Peter*, a fishing vessel that made her home in Stonington port, was a vessel with a rich history. Built at Franklin Post Yard in nearby Mystic, she was a small ship that would, on occasion, struggle to fish, due to the strong New England winds and tides pushing her back toward the shore. Manuel Madeira, an immigrant from Portugal, purchased her for $500 in 1918, or just over $8,500 today. She was 75 feet long and was used primarily for mackerel fishing, which required two hands. Madeira would fish on the boat until 1949. He died in 1954 and is buried next to his beloved wife, Connie, in St. Mary's Cemetery. (Courtesy of the Stonington Historical Society.)

This photograph shows the steamer *Gladys* in port in Stonington. She was a 55-foot cabin steam launch and was purchased for $2,300 (over $63,000 today) in September 1904 by the US Department of War to transfer troops between the mainland and Fort Mansfield on Watch Hill in Rhode Island. Fort Mansfield itself was a disaster, as it was so poorly designed that one report stated it could be taken with a fleet of coal barges equipped with rapid-fire guns. Upon the purchase of *Gladys*, she was renamed the *Lieutenant Bernard*. Her later service took her to South Carolina, where she was sold to civilian E.T. Howard. (Courtesy of the Stonington Historical Society.)

Shown here at dock among several smaller boats is the auxiliary sloop *Etta & Lena*. According to *Power Boat News*, she was commissioned by Capt. John Ostman on May 6, 1905. She was 33 feet long, 13 feet wide, and powered by a 10-horsepower Lathrop engine. On May 20, it was reported that Captain Otsman was using her to fish for mackerel off Long Island. On October 7 of that year, Captain Otsman and his crew had caught 32 barrels of mackerel near the East Breakwater. On November 18, the captain fitted her for cruises between Block Island and Montauk. Needless to say, *Etta & Lena* got around! (Courtesy of the Stonington Historical Society.)

Shown here in dock at Stonington in front of the old fish market and the Pendelton dry goods store is the auxiliary schooner *Gazelle*. Legend has it that Capt. Ben Chesebrough brought owner John Atwood's schooner to the Harvard-Yale boat races and sailed her backwards down the Thames River. More reliable records show her registered in Stonington in 1904 after being built in Noank in 1896. She was 59 feet long and nearly 18 feet wide. She struggled in strong winds in June 1907 before hiding behind Block Island to weather a storm. She was sold to the US government in 1910. (Courtesy of the Stonington Historical Society.)

Shown here washed ashore during the great Stonington hurricane of 1938 is the fishing vessel *Bertha-C*. She was owned by Manuel, a Portuguese immigrant who is mentioned elsewhere in this book. She is listed in *Merchant Vessels of the United States* in 1948 and 1950, so there is little doubt that she was refloated after the storm. One of the more exciting moments in her years of service at sea was on October 5, 1946, when the crew recovered a torpedo at sea. The torpedo was towed to Longos Dock, and the US Navy installations at New London and Newport were put on alert. (Courtesy of the Stonington Historical Society.)

Shown here as she departs the port at Stonington for a fishing expedition is the *Little Chief*. Constructed in 1945, *Little Chief* was one of the first boats built at Stonington Boat Works, which was opened by Henry R. Palmer in 1938. At 21 gross tons and 47 feet, she was well-equipped to fish the waters of Long Island Sound. She was recorded again at dock in Stonington in 1955. William I. Bomster, a longtime deckhand who passed away in 2019, counted the *Little Chief* as one of many boats he worked on under Capt. Jimmy Henry. (Courtesy of the Stonington Historical Society.)

Shown here in Stonington Harbor is the schooner *William H. Draper*. After starting life as the *Charlotte W. Miller*, in 1919 she was purchased at a US marshal's sale, having been sunk by a submarine in 1917 and renamed after the man who bought the most shares in her. She was 128 feet long and nearly 33 feet wide, 9 feet deep, and weighed 242 tons. Later that year, she was purchased by the New Bedford Dry Dock Company and was scheduled to make a run to Madagascar. On May 12, 1922, she was caught with several illegal immigrants below deck, as there was a demand for cheap labor that saw such ships used to run immigrants. She was abandoned in Camocim, Brazil, in 1924. (Courtesy of the Stonington Historical Society.)

This photograph by Richard Mei shows the pride of Stonington: its industrial fishing fleet. The caption reads: "Part of the Stonington, Connecticut fishing fleet rests in port on a foggy morning in November. The state's last fishing fleet, known as the Southern New England Fishermens and Lobstermens Association, included more than 50 boats when it was formed December 4, 1931. Now, there are 30. Stonington seafarers descended from a seafaring tradition begun by intrepid Yankee traders in clipper ships." (Collection of M. Earl Smith.)

This 1985 Alexander Day photograph shows one of the harsh realities of living on the coast: storm damage. This 35-foot sailboat was one of many washed up on the rocks in Stonington Harbor by Hurricane Gloria. She is pictured being salvaged by Gallup Marine Services of Point Judith, Rhode Island. The boat was a total loss. (Collection of M. Earl Smith.)

Shown here are several boats in Stonington Harbor, including the *Black Whale* and *Matthew Mark*. Taken by Stephen Dunn, this photograph was used in newspapers around the country. The Harbor Edge condominiums are visible in the background. (Collection of M. Earl Smith.)

Shown here in Stonington Harbor is the schooner *Andrew Nebinger*. She ran aground on January 27, 1919, while making a voyage from Jacksonville, Florida, to Banes, Cuba, just three miles from her destination. The schooner also ran aground on a reef in 1915 and had to be aided by another ship. The crew members, it seems, brought a lot of bad luck on themselves. In one instance, she was towed to sea only to find she had no fresh water onboard. (Courtesy of the Southwest Harbor Public Library.)

This drawing, showing the Stonington fishing vessels *Marise* and *Two Brothers* in dock at Stonington Harbor, was drawn by artist Richard Welling and bears a close resemblance to one in his 1974 book *Drawing with Markers*. Welling donated a large portion of his Connecticut work to the Connecticut Historical Society. A veteran of World War II, his most famous works are his numerous drawings of the New York skyline, in particular a series depicting the World Trade Center under construction. Welling passed away in 2009. (Courtesy of the Connecticut Historical Society.)

Shown here on their boat *Freedom* are the Miller family, Thomas, Lynn, Lloyd, Brice, and Lindsay, in the late 1950s. Thomas Lloyd Miller was a retired commander in the US Navy who opened the Miller Ford Company in Stonington. The family moved to Coconut Grove, Florida, in 1963. He passed away in 1985. Lindsay married E. Garrett Colson Jr. on September 9, 1971, an event that was covered by the *New York Times*. Bruce passed away on August 30, 2013, after a battle with cancer. (Courtesy of the Stonington Historical Society.)

The nitrate hauler *Anne R. Wood* is in port at Stonington. Nitrate has many uses, including as a fertilizer and an explosive. One of its other uses is as a food preservative, which would make sense for Stonington, as the port was serviced by a fish market, and dried seafood was in high demand. Transport of nitrate is tricky, so doing it by sea made sense, as the material is water soluble, which would inhibit an explosion in case of an accident. (Courtesy of the Stonington Historical Society.)

This photograph shows the fishing vessel *Weir* docked in Stonington, an American flag fluttering proudly in the breeze. Although there are no registration records of this boat, its name could come from two sources. There is a Weir family with a storied history in Stonington, with Thomas Weir named secretary of the Community Club on February 3, 1921, and John D. Weir opening the Lantern Hill Silica Company. In the fishing world, a weir is an obstruction placed in the opening of a river or bay meant to direct fish into nets or traps. (Courtesy of the Stonington Historical Society.)

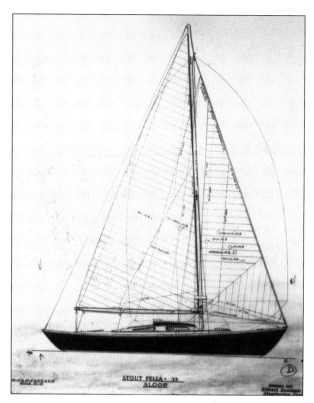

This design schematic, donated by renowned Stonington photographer Maurice La Gura, shows a Stout Fella sailboat with a sloop rig. La Gura was born in Stonington to Italian parents on Christmas Eve in 1914. After earning two Purple Hearts at Normandy, he returned to Stonington, married, and settled into a life of photography. The Stout Fella was created by W. Gilbert Dunham and was his best-known design. (Courtesy of the Stonington Historical Society.)

This is another schematic of a Stout Fella, this one with a yawl rig. Dunham was at various times during his career a partner with Dunham & Stadel and Dunham & Timken. He designed the yacht *Palmer Johnson* in 1967, and the last boat he designed was the *Firebird*, a large aluminum ketch built for his business partner John Timken. His boats were constructed by Mystic Shipyards in Mystic and Sturgeon Bay Boat Works, which built his Stout Fellas almost exclusively after World War II. (Courtesy of the Stonington Historical Society.)

Pictured on the Groton shoreline of the Mystic River is the trolley car house and powerhouse of the Groton & Stonington Street Railway, chartered in 1903. The trolley line traversed what is known today as Mystic, connecting the towns of Groton to Stonington; later, sections were added to connect New London, Old Mystic, and Westerly, Rhode Island. The trolleys ceased operations in 1928, replaced by buses run by the Groton-Stonington Traction Company. Today, the buildings are luxury condominiums on Water Street. (Courtesy of the Library of Congress.)

VIEW OF
STONINGTON, CONN.
O. H. BAILEY & CO., PUBLISHERS, BOSTON.
1879.

This 1879 bird's-eye view of Long Point (today's Stonington Point) features landmarks featured throughout this publication, including the steamboat *Stonington* (left foreground, No. 4); the Stonington Lighthouse and Signal Station, known today as the Old Lighthouse Museum (far right, No. 15); the "old cemetery," 200-plus years old and now known as the Captain Thomas Robinson Burying Ground, the only cemetery on Stonington Point (far left near the corner of Water and Broad Streets); and the Episcopal church, built in 1849 and known now as Calvary Church (top center, No. 10). (Courtesy of the Boston Public Library.)

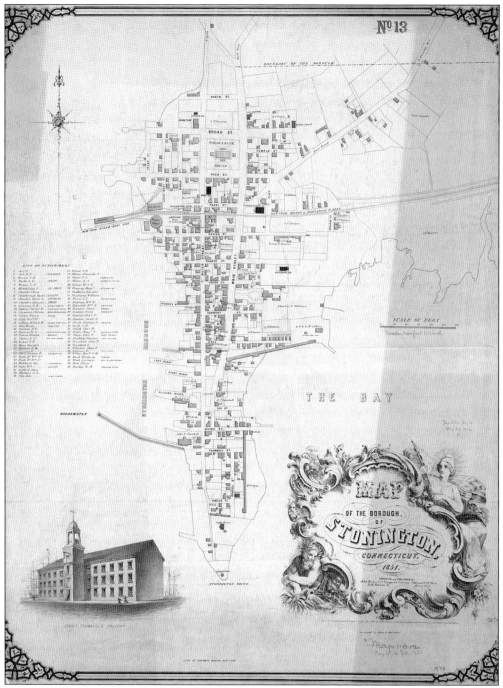

Printed in 1851, this map shows the borough of Stonington. In 1724, the town of North Stonington was set off from the rest of the area and incorporated into its own town in 1807. John Bevan, a civil engineer and surveyor based in New York City and Jersey City, New Jersey, published this map. The actual surveying of the town was done by John F. Harrison. Several family names, including Denison, Collins, Williams, and Hyde, are assigned to plots. (Courtesy of the Boston Public Library.)

On November 12, 1858, the New Haven, New London, and Stonington Railroad Company broke ground on the Stonington Depot, on what had been Samuel F. Denison's saltworks. In 1861, a dedicated wire was run to conduct business with the outside world. C.B. States started transporting people to and from the depot in 1875. The depot is shown here looking west toward New London in 1897. It burned down on February 11, 1897, after a break-in and was rebuilt by Atwood W. Brayton. (Courtesy of the Stonington Historical Society.)

Shown here on a blustery November 8, 1974, is the Amtrak train "Yankee Clipper" passing through Stonington on the old New Haven "Shore Line." The photograph was taken by Ronald N. Johnson. (Collection of M. Earl Smith.)

This is part of Amtrak's Northeast Corridor through Stonington. The corridor from Washington, DC, to Boston see nearly 2,200 trains and 12 million passengers a day. (Collection of M. Earl Smith.)

This image shows the now closed track crossing at Water Street, just past the Wadawanuck Club in Stonington. The crossing was closed in 1999 due to the installation of a power generating station, which made the rail for all of Amtrak's Northeast Corridor electric. The Stonington station, as a paralleling station, was installed at mile marker 134.7. (Collection of M. Earl Smith.)

Two

A King and His Castle

Landmarks and Homes of Stonington

Located on Little Narragansett Bay on Green Haven Road in the Pawcatuck section of Stonington, the Robert Stanton House is the oldest building in Stonington, dating to the 1670s. It was constructed by Stonington founder Thomas Stanton and came to also be named for the Davis family, who ran the homestead as a farm from 1772 to the late 20th century. During the American Revolution, the farm produced salt hay to feed Continental army horses. It was selected as the home of the Stanton-Davis Homestead Museum, which was founded in 2004 but has not yet opened due to lack of funding. (Courtesy of the Library of Congress.)

The Amos Palmer House was built in the Georgian style in 1787 after its predecessor was destroyed by a neighbor's barn fire. The home was constructed by and for Capt. Amos Palmer, a descendant of one of the founding fathers of Stonington, Walter Palmer. Despite taking cannon fire during the War of 1812, the home stands today, having played host to, among others, artist James McNeill Whistler, Pulitzer Prize winner Stephen Vincent Benet, and Canadian artist, designer, children's book author, and filmmaker James Archibald Houston. (Collection of M. Earl Smith.)

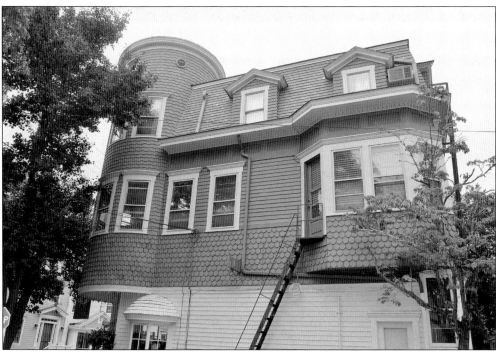

Shown here is the James Merrill House at 107 Water Street. In 1954, Merrill moved with his partner David Jackson to this house, where he spent his summers for the next 41 years until his death in 1995. It was here that his most important literary work, *The Changing Light at Sandover*, was composed. A book-length epic poem, it was claimed to be based on conversations that Merrill and Jackson had with the spirit world through a Ouija board. It is now the home of the James Merrill Writer-in-Residence Program. (Collection of M. Earl Smith.)

This is James Merrill's bed at the James Merrill House. His 1976 collection of poetry, *Divine Comedies*, was also written using notes from his sessions with a Ouija board. Merrill thought he was speaking to people from the past, including poet W.H. Auden (who had passed away in 1973) and filmmaker Maya Deren. Despite the controversy surrounding its creation, the volume won the 1977 Pulitzer Prize for poetry. (Collection of M. Earl Smith.)

Wequetequock Burial Ground is one of the earliest cemeteries in Stonington. The first burial was nine-year-old Joseph Chesebrough in 1650, who was mowing grass with a scythe in a marsh when he was accidentally cut and bled to death. In November 1651, Walter Palmer was buried here. Thomas Miner, also buried on the grounds, has a wolf stone covering his grave to keep the beasts from stealing his body. (Courtesy of Robert Stanton.)

The Captain Nathaniel B. Palmer House sits at 40 Palmer Street in Stonington, a mere stones' throw from the borough and the sea. It was built by Nathaniel Brown Palmer, an explorer of the Antarctic, seal hunter, and designer of clipper ships. Threatened with demolition in 1994, the house was purchased by the Stonington Historical Society to be used as a museum dedicated to the life, times, and accomplishments of Captain Palmer. Occupying a four-acre lot, the home was listed in the National Register of Historic Places in 1996. (Collection of M. Earl Smith.)

This house in Stonington was the home of Edward Darrell and his family. On July 29, 1899, Darrell was elected the first president of the Wadawanuck Golf Club. On August 3, 1901, he was named to a search committee for the site of a country club. On July 19, he purchased a lot for the club. In 1920, he and his wife celebrated their 25th anniversary at their summer home at Cove Lawn. In a friendly race on August 5, 1922, his sailboat *Ace* defeated the *Toxeuna*, owned by Dr. Charles M. Williams, and the *Imp*, owned by Charles H. Simmons. (Courtesy of the Stonington Historical Society.)

This house has been known at various times as the Peleg Brown House and the Wampossett Inn. It was started by Capt. Peleg Brown, who died in 1796 and did not live to see its completion in 1798. Brown was an early slave owner in Stonington, leaving his slave Phyllis to his wife after his passing. Brown's daughter married Capt. Nathaniel Palmer, who named Palmerland in the Antarctic. For years, the house stored Palmer's records and log books, even after a move from 96 to 94 Water Street. It is currently a private residence. (Courtesy of the Stonington Historical Society.)

Shown here during the ownership of Harriet Trumbull Palmer is 25 High Street, built by local legend John F. Trumbull. He was born on July 21, 1796, in Norwich and was elected a representative of Stonington in 1838 and reelected in 1856, 1859, and 1864. In 1849, he owned most of the land on Trumbull Street. Trumbull helped charter Stonington Savings Bank, and built a horse nail factory on Water Street. In June 1861, he opened the Joslyn Rifle Factory, which supplied arms to the Union during the Civil War. He passed away in 1874. (Courtesy of the Stonington Historical Society.)

This photograph is part of a series by Robert Brewster for the Historic American Buildings Survey, which documents historical districts across the United States. This one records the Wilcox Road Historic District in the Lords Point section of Stonington. It is titled, "View from end of James Avenue, Lord's Point, looking northwest towards Wilcox Road Historic District." James Avenue is now James Street and runs from the west, intersecting Walnut Street, Quarry Path, Noyes Avenue, Boulder Avenue, Langworthy Avenue, and Ashworth Avenue before terminating at Wolcott Avenue. (Courtesy of the Library of Congress.)

This is a view from the Amtrak railroad overpass at Noyes Avenue, looking west toward the Wilcox Road Historic District. Noyes Avenue reaches to the houses at the end of the point before intersecting Quarry Path, James Street, Boulder Avenue, and Lindberg Avenue and then terminating inland at Lords Hill Road. (Courtesy of the Library of Congress.)

This picture from the Wilcox Road Historic District Survey is titled "View from U.S. Route 1, looking southwest over Quiambog Cove towards Wilcox Road Historic District." Quiambaug Cove is an important part of Stonington lore. Thomas Miner built his home i on Quiambaug, and a diary detailing his early life there is available digitally, in part, through George Mason University. The area was also one of the top commercial oyster producers in Connecticut in 1900. It is roughly one sixth of the town's land area. (Courtesy of the Library of Congress.)

The Miner Cemetery, across from Quiambaug Cove, was founded by Thomas Miner. It is seen here from the Route 1 bridge over the cove. The cemetery contains roughly 100 graves, with the vast majority belonging to the Miner family. Among them is Thomas Miner, the first Miner in Stonington, who was interred here in 1760. Two Native Americans, Cato and Plato, are buried here as well, having been workers on the Miner farm. (Courtesy of the Library of Congress.)

This view of Latimer Point from the Wilcox Road Historic District survey is titled "View from beach, looking southwest over railroad tracks towards Latimer Point." Today, Latimer Point is a hotspot for real estate and a popular site for vacation homes. On the west side of the point are views of Masons Island, while on the east, Long Island Sound and Fishers Island can be seen. At the end of the point is a small strait separating the mainland from Andrews Island. (Courtesy of the Library of Congress.)

Latimer Point is seen in this photograph from the Historic American Buildings Survey. According to the Library of Congress, the Wilcox Road Historic District contains a significant concentration of late 19th and early 20th century residential buildings "in a rare, well-preserved rural coastal setting." The district is on a point surrounded by water on three sides, with historic buildings dating from 1874 to c. 1940. (Courtesy of the Library of Congress.)

This photograph from the Historic American Buildings Survey for the Wilcox Road Historic District shows Fisher Island Sound from the intersection of Route 1 and Wilcox Road looking south. Fisher Island Sound has managed to avoid the crowds of tourists present in other waterways in the area, such as the congested Long Island Sound, because there is no place on Fisher Island for visitors to stay. The island is inhabited strictly by homeowners. (Courtesy of the Library of Congress.)

This image is titled "View from Amtrak Railroad tracks, looking east along tracks towards Wilcox Road Historic District." According to the Library of Congress, "the period of significance for the district extends from 1760, the date of the oldest stone in the Miner Cemetery, to 1948." (Courtesy of the Library of Congress.)

This is a view from the north end of Latimer Point looking northeast. According to the Library of Congress, most of the contributing buildings in the Wilcox Road Historic District are associated with members of the Wilcox family and "retain their historic architectural appearance to a high degree." The Amtrak rails cross the district near the southern tip of Quiambaug Neck and separate the houses from the water. (Courtesy of the Library of Congress.)

This aerial view shows the Pawcatuck Hurricane Protection Barrier, which runs along the border of Pawcatuck and Stonington. Completed in September 1963, it cost $859,000 and is the responsibility of Stonington. According to the US Army Corps of Engineers, it consists of 1,915 feet of earth fill dike and 940 feet of concrete wall, both with an elevation of 17 feet. (Courtesy of the US Army Corps of Engineers.)

The Pawcatuck River flows through the Pawcatuck section of Stonington into Little Narragansett Bay at the Rhode Island border. The river is 34 miles long and meanders through Rhode Island before winding along the border of Connecticut for the rest of its path. No less than eight dams have dotted its length, and the US Navy replenishment oil tanker USS *Pawcatuck* gets its name from the river. (Courtesy of the US Army Corps of Engineers.)

Stonington Harbor is west of Stonington on the north shore of Fishers Island Sound. This aerial photograph is from July 1983 and shows the west side of the harbor, where most of the boats come in past Stonington Point. Aerial photographs like these help the US Army Corps of Engineers prepare for possible damage from hurricanes and other storms. (Courtesy of the US Army Corps of Engineers.)

Here is another aerial view of Stonington Harbor from July 1983. The harbor is on the north shore of Fisher Island Sound, which opens to the Atlantic Ocean. (Courtesy of the US Army Corps of Engineers.)

With a population of nearly 20,000, there is plenty of use for the harbor in Stonington. In addition to a fishing fleet, the harbor hosts a great deal of pleasure and sailing crafts as well as businesses tailored to the construction, building, maintenance, and repair of boats and boating accessories. (Courtesy of the US Army Corps of Engineers.)

Shown here at right next to what is now Dime Bank is the Gilbert Collins House. It was built in 1853 for Gilbert William Collins, who in partnership with his brother Daniel and Mark Glines ran a business that produced doors and window sashes. The house overlooks Cannon Square, which commemorates the Battle of Stonington during the War of 1812. (Courtesy of the Stonington Historical Society.)

Walnut Grove, the 85-acre estate of James Ingersoll Day, is seen here in the beautiful desolation of a coastal New England winter. By 1888, the estate had passed to Chas P. Palmer, who constructed a private racetrack there. On August 4, 1888, a race between a father and son attracted 1,000 spectators. In 1911, owner Thomas R. Manners sold the estate to Mary Eliza and Emmabel H. Heath and Annette S. Norton, who built the Stonington Manor Inn on the site, which is north and west of Lambert's Cove between North Main and North Water Streets. (Courtesy of the Stonington Historical Society.)

The carriage of Dr. Charles P. Williams carries four of Stonington's elite past Matthews Park, on the old salt flats across from the railroad depot. The land was purchased by the Stonington Village Improvement Association for $1 in 1947. Today, the park hosts an annual ice cream social on the Fourth of July, with free ice cream courtesy of the Dogwatch Café. Dodson Boatyard takes care of all trash in the park, free of charge. The park, while public, can be reserved for private events for a modest fee. (Courtesy of the Stonington Historical Society.)

This was the house of Fredrick "Fred" Chesebro, born in Stonington on October 20, 1805, to Elder Elihu and Lydia Chesebro. This house replaced the one that was built when the family first occupied the land in 1649. Fred Chesebro attended school until he was 16 and then became a farmer. He married Mary A. Chesebro on October 25, 1837, and they had five children. Chesebro was a registered Democrat all of his life and outlived four of his five children and his wife. (Courtesy of the Stonington Historical Society.)

This is the former house of Jabaz Chesebro, a descendent of Fred Chesebro and a direct descendent of one of the four founding fathers of Stonington. Jabaz was born on May 11, 1847, in Stonington. He lived here at 66 Elm Street with his wife, Etta, who he married on March 12, 1873; son William, who died as a teenager in 1893 while studying to become a pharmacist; and daughter Grace. Jabaz belonged to the Independent Order of Odd Fellows and was a member of the Stonington Baptist Church. (Courtesy of the Stonington Historical Society.)

This view of Main Street is looking south from Cannon Square around 1881. The first house on the left is 7 Main Street, which is a bright yellow home today. Main Street is then intersected by Ash Street on the left. 3 Main Street is the next house on the left. The last house on the street, also on the left, is 1 Main Street, a large five-bedroom home. Main Street ends at the intersection with Diving Street. (Courtesy of the Stonington Historical Society.)

This home on Church Street was once occupied by Frank Watson. He was born in 1840 and worked as a teamster. He also lived in Groton for a time. His wife, Melinda, was a homemaker. Both Frank and Melinda were born in Connecticut, as were both of their parents. The census records that would have included the greatest amount of detail about their lives in Stonington—1890—was destroyed in a fire. (Courtesy of the Stonington Historical Society.)

This is the home of Gilbert Collins on what is now Stonington-Mystic Road. Collins, after leaving Yale for financial reasons in 1862, relocated to Jersey City, New Jersey, in 1863. He practiced law, lost a New Jersey Senate bid in 1880, and then won election as mayor of Jersey City in 1884, serving one term. In 1892, he was a delegate to the Republican National Convention. In 1897, he was appointed to the New Jersey Supreme Court and served until 1903. He died in 1920 and is buried in Hilliard Cemetery in Stonington. (Courtesy of the Stonington Historical Society.)

These are the remains of a home owned by Charles Stanton on Sal Tinkers Hill. In 1658, part of the land on the hill was given to James Avery by a Mr. Thompson, who was working under the authority of a Mr. Tinkers. In 1849, mapmakers for the borough gave the street that ran along the hill the name Cliff, which it carries to this day. In 1873, an order was issued to lock up for the night any child sliding down Sal Tinkers Hill, or any other hill, on the Sabbath. (Courtesy of the Stonington Historical Society.)

Beginning sometime around 1930, Stiles Gilmore lived at 19 Elm Street with his sister Rose. He was born in Ireland and served as an undertaker while he lived in the borough. Rose was listed as the head of the household. In 1903, Stiles was one of the founding members of the Young Men's Catholic Club, where he served as treasurer. (Courtesy of the Stonington Historical Society.)

A barn is being moved from the lot at 178 Water Street, across from Matthews Park and the library. That lot today is occupied by a two-story yellow house. There are several mature maple and birch trees on the property. In addition to serving as a residence, the home is the headquarters of Alexander and Associates, a marketing consulting firm. (Courtesy of the Stonington Historical Society.)

Stonington, due to its location on a peninsula, makes for a dashing subject when it comes to aerial views. Photographer B.L. Gordon knew this, and took this and many similar images for the Book & Tackle Shop in Watch Hill, Rhode Island. (Collection of M. Earl Smith.)

The first graduating class of Stonington High School was in 1875, and the first classes were taught under the guidance of principal George O. Hopkins. On September 6, 1910, the building pictured here opened with 150 students. Clarence E. Sibley was the first principal at the new location, and students from out in the borough came by trolley. In October 1914, Carols A. Woodworth was named the first superintendent of Stonington schools. In 1920, the average local high school teacher earned $1,100 a year. On June 24, 1926, the Stonington Historical Society awarded cash prizes to two high school students for their essays on lighthouses. (Collection of M. Earl Smith.)

47

"THE HILL" STONINGTON, CONN.

"The Hill" first entered history in 1789, when Rev. Hezekiah Woodruff, who was minister of the Road Church until 1803, built a house here. The home was later occupied by Samuel F. Dennison and Edward P. York. In 1818, Dennison was named selectman, and in 1819, he was elected state representative for Stonington. Later that year, he helped form the Asylum Lodge No. 57 of Free and Accepted Masons. In 1824, he was one of the managers of Stonington Academy. York was a New York architect who summered in Stonington and died on December 30, 1928, at age 63. (Collection of M. Earl Smith.)

This aerial view of Stonington was published by the Book & Tackle Shop in Watch Hill. (Collection of M. Earl Smith.)

What is now known as the Horace Niles Trumbull House on the corner of Main and Broad Streets in Stonington was constructed in 1860 by businessman John F. Trumbull for his son Horace and family. The mansion is built in the Italiantine and French Second Empire style. Since 1899, the home has belonged to the family of Josiah Culbert Palmer. (Collection of M. Earl Smith.)

This Frank J. Raymond photograph shows Stonington's fishing fleet. The fleet has had several ups and downs in the last several years. In 2017, it faced what promised to be near disastrous cuts in fluke quotas. In 2019, Gov. Ned Lamont signed a bill that allowed any vessel with a license from Connecticut, New York, or Rhode Island to register a catch in any Connecticut port, from the coastal waters of any of the three states, without penalty. (Collection of M. Earl Smith.)

This is the dining room of the Captain Amos Sheffield House. Constructed by the captain in 1765, it stands on the corner of Water and Wall Streets in Stonington. The front has a double set of steps. His daughter married merchant Enoch S. Chesebrough, who had the house raised to accommodate a variety store in the basement. As with many of the historic homes in Stonington, the house has a historical marker. (Collection of M. Earl Smith.)

Pictured is the home of Rev. James Noyes II, founder of the Congregational Church in Stonington. In addition to his duties as a reverend, Noyes was one of 10 men responsible for the founding of Yale University in New Haven. His name is one of 10 engraved on Woodbridge Hall at Yale. He was also the son-in-law of Thomas Stanton, the namesake of the Thomas Stanton Society. In 1690, Stonington built a small house for Noyes to warm himself between morning and afternoon services. He is buried in Wequetequock Cemetery in Stonington. (Collection of M. Earl Smith.)

The Stonington Lighthouse, shown here with its famous "washbowl" boulder in front, had seven keepers during its 49 years of service: William Potter; his widow, Patty B. Potter; Luther Ripley; Winthrop Hand; Henry Burgess; Charles E.P. Noyes; and Capt. Benjamin F. Pendelton. The property was listed in the National Register of Historic Places in 1976. (Collection of M. Earl Smith.)

This is the beautiful spiral staircase in the Stanton Homestead, which is now the property of the Thomas Stanton Society. The home was managed and owned by Whit Davis, who delighted in showing off the staircase, which had been imported from England and placed in the 300-year-old home. After one of the reunions of the Thomas Stanton Society, Davis donated the property to the nonprofit, ensuring its preservation for generations to come. The society works today to fulfill that goal. (Collection of M. Earl Smith.)

Portuguese immigrants of Stonington used Cannon Square to show their loyalty to their new nation on October 20, 1918. While their Portuguese heritage was honored, there could be little doubt that the ceremony was a profound moment of patriotism for these new citizens. (Collection of M. Earl Smith.)

This postcard features the crown jewel of the Stonington Historical Society's holdings, the Lighthouse Museum. The lighthouse was erected in 1841 to replace an older tower on the point. This photograph by Bernard L. Gordon was published by the Book & Tackle Shop in Watch Hill. (Collection of M. Earl Smith.)

This postcard, dated September 17, 1907, was sent from Stonington to Edna M. Round in Anthony, Rhode Island. It was published by the German-owned Rotograph Company of New York City. The message reads, "I came ashore to see cousin Cliff. Each Sun. and expect to stay until Wednesday. We were out again yesterday and had a good time. These cannons are historic, you know." The writer, it seems, had a talent for understatement. (Collection of M. Earl Smith.)

Although their design has changed, the Amos Palmer House still features dual staircases to this day. Whistler is not the only artist of repute to inhabit the home. Stephen Vincent Benet purchased the house in 1940, and his descendants lived there from his death in 1943 until 1983. (Collection of M. Earl Smith.)

This postcard is titled "Birds Eye View of Stonington, Conn. Looking East." As of the 2010 Census, the population of Stonington was 18,545, which represented a 3.6 percent growth from 2000. (Collection of M. Earl Smith.)

Three

RUGGED INDIVIDUALISM

BUSINESS AND CAPITALISM IN STONINGTON

First National Bank, seen here in 1940 from Cannon Square (also known as Town Square, which was constructed at the same time as the bank), was established as Ocean Bank in 1851. In 1865, the bank became nationalized with the doubling of its capital from $100,000 to $200,000. In 1942, the building was purchased by the Stonington Historical Society to house its headquarters, but World War II necessitated its lease to the American Red Cross. The building today is the home of Dime Bank. (Courtesy of the Library of Congress.)

Dodson Boatyard currently has 112 moorings of its own, in addition to 85 private moorings. It was acquired by the Snyder family in 1980. In 2015, the boatyard started its own in-house sail and canvas care facility. The boatyard provides emergency, on-water service through its service vessel, the M/V *Alert*, which logged 286 hours of service calls during the 2016 boating season. Dodson has a tradition of gifting its employees a Rolex watch upon the completion of 20 years of service. (Collection of M. Earl Smith.)

Shown here with patrons Charlie Burtch (a selectman) and Harry Pendelton in the doorway, the Arcade Building at 61–65 Water Street has served many purposes. Today, it is owned by the Stonington Historical Society and serves as apartments and offices for Dime Bank. It was also used to film scenes in the 1988 Julia Roberts film *Mystic Pizza*. In its past it housed a grocery store, a cabinet-making shop, a machine shop, a butcher shop, a fish market, a candy store, a bookstore, and a doll shop. (Courtesy of the Stonington Historical Society.)

This is the machine shop run by Alex P. Loper, an engineer and inventor responsible for numerous innovations. In 1891, he was one of the founding members of the Wadawanuck Tennis Club. In 1898, he was granted a patent for a device that would control the engine from the pilot house on a boat. In 1900, the borough purchased a fire suppression system that Loper invented. Mystic purchased a similar system in 1915. In 1925, Loper became president of the Stonington Fire District. A new fire suppression system was sold to a firm in Chicago in 1929 for $250,000. (Courtesy of the Stonington Historical Society.)

Shown here is 70 Water Street in Stonington, famous for being one of the shooting locales for *Mystic Pizza*. All of the interior scenes of the pizzeria were shot here. Today, the building is one of two used by the New England Science and Sailing Foundation (the other is 72 Water Street). Founded in 2002 by the Stonington Harbor Yacht Club, the foundation seeks to offer community sailing programs based on seamanship, sportsmanship, safety, and fun. (Collection of M. Earl Smith.)

Construction for the Stonington Post Office began in 1940 as a federal works project and was completed in 1941. Louis A. Simon was the supervising architect, and Neal A. Melick was the supervising engineer. The post office serves the 06355, 06372, 06378, 06379, and 06388 zip codes. (Collection of M. Earl Smith.)

The old Stonington High School, not to be confused with the current Stonington High School in Pawcatuck, was constructed in 1888 at 25 Orchard Street. The building is a fine example of Second Empire architecture. Atwood W. Brayton and Lorenzo H. Lamb were the architects. This building was listed in the National Register of Historic Places in 1978. It has since been converted to residential use. (Collection of M. Earl Smith.)

First Stonington Conn. Bank, Charter 1822 "Custom House"

The First National Bank of Stonington went into voluntary liquidation on February 24, 1940, with its last president being J. Rodney Smith. The Great Depression saw over 9,000 banks fail, with a loss of $125 billion in depositor assets. This building was purchased on October 1, 1941, by the Stonington Historical Society. (Courtesy of the Library of Congress.).

Sailor Ed's was on Route 1 entering Stonington from Mystic at 29 Old Stonington Road. Alice L. Burdick, who passed away in 2008 at the age of 94, was a waitress there. An image of Capt. Charles Fowler hung in the restaurant for years. It was robbed on September 24, 1972, at 10:00 p.m. The eastern Connecticut chapter of the American Association of Occupational Health Nurses held its annual meeting there on May 23, 1979. In 1996, Sailor Ed's became the Quiambaug House, owned by Ainslie and George Turner. The building is now vacant, having hosted a nightclub called Tongue and Groove for a time. (Courtesy of the Stonington Historical Society.)

This is Byron J. Gardiner's dry goods store. Gardiner was born on August 9, 1854, in Rhode Island. He was one of four men who founded the Pioneer Hook and Ladder Company on March 5, 1884. Gardiner was a candidate three times for state representative for the Prohibition Party (1894, 1904, and 1906). He was a member of the Second Congregational Church, and his wife's composition cake is in the church's 1911 recipe book. In 1904, his son Henry narrowly escaped injury after colliding on his bike with the Arcade grocery wagon. Gardiner passed away November 17, 1928, and is buried in Evergreen Cemetery. (Courtesy of the Stonington Historical Society.)

Located at 105 Water Street is the Hungry Palette, a fabric and clothing store that presents itself as a dry goods store. The shop has been in business for over 41 years and offers a wide variety of fabrics as well as clothing and paintings. The fabrics are the heart of the business and are all made on-site and by hand. (Courtesy of the Library of Congress.)

BARRAZAstyle is the retail outlet of fashion designer Maria Barraza at 107 Water Street in Stonington. Barraza has worked with many famous names, including Tipper Gore, CNN's Soledad O'Brien, and ABC anchor Elizabeth Vargas. (Courtesy of the Library of Congress.)

A Stonington institution, Noah's Restaurant at 113 Water Street celebrated its 40th year of serving up incredible meals in August 2019. The 75 seats limit crowds, and the spot is popular for filming; scenes from the 2019 Hallmark film *Holiday for Heroes* were shot here. The restaurant is open Tuesday through Sunday. (Courtesy of the Library of Congress.)

Located at 134 Water Street is Indigo Bleu, an upscale boutique that offers a wide variety of clothing and accessories. The boutique takes pride in its wide variety of items made in the United States, its fair trade items, and its wide variety of accessories. The store is a member of the Fair Trade Federation. (Courtesy of the Library of Congress.)

Next Interior Design is at 135 Water Street, and A.K. Dasher Jewelry and Gifts is next door at 141 Water Street. Next has appeared in several top 10 lists of Stonington designers, dating to 1998. A.K. Dasher is an eclectic shop, hosting both traditional jewelry and gifts. It is said to be one of the largest sterling silver jewelers in New England and received praise from periodicals such as the *Boston Globe*. It is open from 10:00 a.m. to 6:00 p.m. seven days a week. (Courtesy of the Library of Congress.)

This photograph shows two businesses on Water Street. Philip Darrell Lighting Design, which shares its building with Black Orchid Jewelry, is at 119B Water Street. The business next door at 117 Water Street used to be a barbershop but is now home to Social Coffee Roastery. (Courtesy of the Library of Congress.)

Formerly La Grua's, the building at 121 Water Street is now Gallery 121, an upscale art gallery that opened in 2017. Established by Briggs Whiteford, Gallery 121's mission is to encourage creative expression in everyday life. (Courtesy of the Library of Congress.)

The Wadawanuck Club was founded in the early 1900s as the Wadawanuck Tennis Club by members including Edward F. Darrell, Charles H. Simmons, J. Culbert Palmer, and Judge Gilbert C. Collins. Its entrance is seen here in a Rollie McKenna photograph taken in the off-season. It moved from a modest clubhouse on Water Street in 1914 to Nat's Point, which was leased to the club by Capt. Nathaniel Palmer's granddaughter Elisabeth Palmer Loper. Six years later, the Wadawanuck Yacht Club was added. (Courtesy Stonington Historical Society.)

E. Lamphere's Old Mystic delivery van pauses for a photograph in the late 1800s outside of Dr. C.E. Brayton's pharmacy in Stonington. The building that housed the pharmacy still stands at the corner of High and Main Streets. Dr. Brayton was a chemist and physician who ran his shop with C.T. Willard on the lower floor of 77 Main Street. Today, the building houses Realty 3. (Courtesy of Stonington Historical Society.)

This photograph taken by Richard Mei shows fishermen adding ice to fish for shipment on December 7, 1992. (Collection of M. Earl Smith.)

This view is looking north toward the center of town at the corner of Union and Water Streets. Union Street comes to an end at the three-way intersection with Water Street. Many residential homes are seen here, although the building on the corner at right has now been converted to the Hungry Palette, a high-end women's clothing store at 105 Water Street. This has been the fate of many of the old homes in the area. (Courtesy of the Stonington Historical Society.)

The building at 114 Water Street has changed quite a bit since this photograph was taken. The bay window is gone and the front door is now enclaved, with a stoop to keep visitors out of the elements. The use of the building has changed as well. For 26 years, Peter Cummings ran a landscape and design company here before relocating to Fairfield. Today, it is home to Grace Your Home, which was opened in 2019 by Mary Grace Sponn. (Courtesy of the Stonington Historical Society.)

This is one of the many pharmacies that occupied the shop at 101 Main Street at the corner of High Street. It was originally built in 1880 and named the Brayton Building. The first business to occupy the space was Brayton's. Francis J. Connors bought the business after graduating from the Massachusetts College of Pharmacology in 1923, renaming it Connors' Pharmacy. Dr. Connors later took part in Stonington's Ambulance Corps. In 1936, he helped found Stonington's first Boy Scout troop. (Courtesy of the Stonington Historical Society.)

Shown here at 143 Water Street is a pool hall that was owned by the Stanton family. The building was likely damaged by a fire. Billiard halls had little luck in the area, as on March 12, 1893, another billiard hall was destroyed when the Mystic Opera House burned down. On August 1, 1935, John Marino opened a package store here but moved to 151 Water Street 10 months later. Today, Water Street Café occupies this location. (Courtesy of the Stonington Historical Society.)

In 1882, C.S. Ryon opened a livery stable on Elm Street. The property once belonged to the Reynolds family. In 1893, Ryon added a stable on High Street to his holdings. On April 17, 1900, he purchased the former Baptist church on Water Street for $2,500. On December 13, 1912, Ryon took part in the Old Timers Concert for the benefit of the Village Improvement Society. In 1914, the church he purchased was used for an exhibit by the Stonington Historical and Genealogical Society. (Courtesy of the Stonington Historical Society.)

Pictured is a house on Water Street in the 1930s. By far the most economically important street in Stonington, Water Street stretches from Mathews Park and Dodson Boatyard in the north and contains local favorites such as Dog Watch Café, the J. Russell Jinishian Gallery, Milagro Café, A.K. Dasher Jewelry and Gifts, Indigo Bleu, Tom's Newsstand, Phillip Darrell Lighting Design, Noah's, the James Merrill House, the New England Science and Sailing Foundation, the Inn at Stonington, the Stonington Harbor Yacht Club, the Lighthouse Museum, and others. (Courtesy of the Stonington Historical Society.)

This house belonged to Joseph Hammond and was located at 201 Main Street, although the address changed to 201 North Main Street. Hammond was born in 1861, and his wife, Annie, was born in 1863. He was superintendent of the Stonington Water Works. The house, with additions, still stands and is now home to Zack's Bar and Grill. (Courtesy of the Stonington Historical Society.)

Formerly where the rail yard and the steamship yard met, the land pictured here is now home to the Stonington Town Dock, which still serves the fishing fleet as well as the shipyards and pleasure craft that call Stonington home. Construction on the rail yard started under the New York, Providence & Boston Railroad in 1833. Many travelers had to stay in Stonington on their way to either New York or Boston. The rail yard later served businesses that boomed with the arrival of the American Velvet Company. (Courtesy of the Stonington Historical Society.)

The Monsanto waste factory site in Stonington burned on July 3, 2003. The former Atwood Machine Company factory building, also known as the Plax and the Monsanto Mills, was on Water Street. The mill was constructed in 1851 by John F. Turnbull. This postcard was one of the last published by the Book & Tackle Shop in Watch Hill. The photograph was taken by Louise Pittaway. (Collection of M. Earl Smith.)

Although now in Mystic, the Whitehall Mansion got its start as a home in Stonington built by Dr. Dudley Woodbridge in 1771. The property passed to the Rodman family, who lived there until 1852. It was then sold to the Wheeler family, who resided on the property for the next 100 years. Highway expansion threatened the home, so in 1962 Florence Grace Bentley Keach purchased the home, restored it, moved it to its current location in Mystic, and gifted it to the Stonington Historical Society, which used it as its headquarters until 1996. It was converted to a hotel in 1996. (Collection of M. Earl Smith.)

The Greenhaven restaurant was near the Stonington/Pawcatuck line, three miles south of Route 1 and across the river from Westerly, Rhode Island. Overlooking Little Narragansett Bay, it was known for its Greenhaven-style lobster. (Collection of M. Earl Smith.)

Taken from a sailboat in Stonington Harbor, this photograph shows an area of the borough known as Stonington Commons. There is a public walking path that leads to a gazebo, and the commons has an eatery on-site as well as condos. (Collection of M. Earl Smith.)

Seen here are several businesses on Water Street in Mystic, including Roberto Freitas American Antiques and Decorative Furniture, Clad In boutique, Macsea monitoring and maintenance services, Bray Consultants Prudential Connecticut Realty, and the Dennis Sirrine Gallery. Sirrine took the place of the Great American Memorabilia Company in 2018, at 155 Water Street. (Collection of M. Earl Smith.)

This view of Water Street looking north at Church Street shows many businesses. Hunter, Moore, and Stearns occupied the real estate office at 117 Water Street as recently as 2011, although the space is now home to the Social Coffee Roastery. The Water Street Barber Shop remains, as does Philip Darrell Lighting Design, Black Orchid Jewelers, and La Grua. Cummin Associates, a landscape design firm, has been in business at 114 Water Street for over 27 years. (Collection of M. Earl Smith.)

Four

TO EACH HIS OWN

CULTURE AND FUN IN STONINGTON

This rather rustic sign marks the entrance to Boulder Beach, one of six beaches that make up the private village of Lord's Point in Stonington. Only the inhabitants of 200 houses and their guests have access to this area of the coast. The beach runs parallel to Boulder Avenue, a road that marks the entrance to Lord's Point with two giant boulders. The area was known as Boulder Point before being renamed Lord's Point on January 11, 1909, by Jerome S. Anderson, a newspaper editor. (Courtesy of the Library of Congress.)

Built in 1840, the Old Lighthouse Museum at 7 Water Street currently serves as the home of the Stonington Historical Society. Noted for its sturdy yet ornate stone construction, it is the only lighthouse in the borough to face the Atlantic. The lighthouse aided sailors crossing the ever-dangerous Fishers Island Sound. The house originally had a flat roof, but it leaked and had to be replaced after two years. (Courtesy of the Library of Congress.)

Produced sometime between 1915 and 1930, this postcard shows Stonington Harbor filled with sailboats and other vessels. Stonington Harbor remains one of the busiest harbors in New England. Most of the traffic is either fishing craft or personal pleasure craft. Numerous services are available. (Courtesy of the Boston Public Library.)

The Old Lighthouse, Stonington, Conn.

78849

The lighthouse was constructed in 1840 and remained in service until 1889, when it was replaced by beacons on the breakwaters of Stonington Harbor. The building housed lightkeepers until 1909 before it was deserted. It was sold by the federal government in 1925 for $3,650, or roughly $53,000 today (a bargain in any era). The property was purchased by the Stonington Historical Society, one of the many fine stewards of history in southeastern Connecticut. (Courtesy of the Boston Public Library.)

Constructed in 1901, St. Mary's Roman Catholic Church is at 22 Broad Street. The parish was originally formed in 1851. The first pastor was Rev. P. Duffy. The church is known for its annual Blessing of the Fleet, which honors the memory of fishermen who have died at sea and blesses the current fleet for safety and success. The first Blessing of the Fleet took place on July 1, 1956, inspired by traditions introduced by Portuguese immigrants to Stonington. (Collection of M. Earl Smith.)

Although sources give four different possible years, contemporary accounts have settled on 1955 as the date for the first Blessing of the Fleet hosted by St. Mary's Church. An anchor-shaped broken wreath of flowers is released, which is blessed and then launched out to sea, as shown here. The day is marked with parades, a 5k run, Mass, a family event, and a concert. (Courtesy of the Stonington Historical Society.)

In September 1887, the members of the Stonington Free Library Association met with the goal of promoting literary interests in Stonington and establishing a library. The library first opened in 1888, and the current library was opened on March 25, 1900. A new section was added to the old building on the north side in 1956. Another addition came in 1990. Today, the Stonington Free Library holds over 33,000 volumes, with 3,300 active cardholders. (Collection of M. Earl Smith.)

Travelers line up to board the ferry to Watch Hill from Stonington at the turn of the 20th century. Watch Hill is on the southwesternmost point of Rhode Island and was once connected to the mainland by Fort Road, which was washed out during the 1938 hurricane. A playground for the elite, the island would often host visitors looking to get away from the high-society hustle and bustle of Stonington and Newport. In the past, the island hosted guests such as Albert Einstein, Henry Ford, Clark Gable, and Groucho Marx. Taylor Swift and Conan O'Brien have owned real estate in the area as well. (Courtesy of the Stonington Historical Society.)

DuBois Beach has long been popular. Today, beachgoers can travel to Stonington village and enjoy a wide variety of seafaring activities, including swimming, crabbing in jetties, picnics under the gazebo, or even tying up their pleasure craft to a small anchor dock. The beach, which is owned by the village and managed by Stonington Community Center, is open from Memorial Day to Labor Day. (Courtesy of the Stonington Historical Society.)

On January 27, 1897, the village of Stonington was hammered by a nor'easter that dumped several inches of snow on the area. This picture was taken on Water Street, south of High Street, after the storm. The old Baptist church building is at left. It was built in 1775, and the first overseer was Pastor John Rathburn. Valentine Rathbun became pastor in 1784 and held the post until 1799. William Gardner headed the church from 1799 to 1802. Elnathan Fellows followed and held the post until 1810. (Courtesy of the Stonington Historical Society.)

Stonington came together on June 1, 1990, to celebrate the 80th birthday of a local legend, Frank M. Keane. Born in Westerly, Keane became a denizen of Stonington at the age of two. At 17, during a fire at the American Oil Company and with his clothes burning, he shut off a gas valve before the blaze could spread. After graduating from high school, he operated Keane's New Office at 133 Water Street for 50 years. He was a member of St. Mary's Church, Stonington's Democratic Town Committee, and Salvation Army and Stonington Draft Board. He passed away in 2000 at 90. (Courtesy of the Stonington Historical Society.)

The white clapboard Road Church building houses the First Congregational Church of Stonington. In 1829, the basement was rented by the Town of Stonington to host the village's first town hall. This is the oldest congregation in Stonington, and the seventh oldest in Connecticut. Located at 903 Pequot Trail, it served as the polling station for the road district until 1967. Each of the four founding families of Stonington has their name listed on a diagram in the church used to indicate reserved seating. (Courtesy of Robert Stanton.)

This photograph, titled "A square with old houses in the old fishing village of Stonington, Connecticut," is perhaps more famous because of who took it than what it shows. It was taken in November 1940 by photographer Jack Delano. Born in Russia, Delano and his family moved to the United States when he was nine. He was a photographer for the Farm Security Administration, a New Deal program that sought to photograph much of rural America. Stonington was one of many villages he photographed. (Courtesy of the Library of Congress.)

Here is another of Delano's photographs, one of 1,600 taken in color by the Farm Security Administration's photographers. According to the Library of Congress, The images offer an insight into America at the time and provided jobs to photographers and other artists during the Great Depression. (Courtesy of the Library of Congress.)

Two women display a flag from the War of 1812 they were repairing for the Stonington tercentenary. A committee was formed during the winter of 1947–1948 to plan the upcoming celebration, consisting of Jerome S. Anderson III, John B. Bindloss, Charles A. Brooks, Griffith Bailey Coale, Clifton Coates, John B. Findlay, Ernest and Ellsworth Gray, Williams Haynes, Otto Liebig, Carroll Peavey, Robert Perkins, Earl B. Lyon, Thomas Stevens, George H. Stone, Aubrey Whitelaw, and Fred Zeller. Many artifacts, including this photograph and a book by William Haynes, stand as memorials to this occasion. (Courtesy of the Stonington Historical Society.)

The Knights of Columbus Hall on Williams Street started life as the Third Baptist Church, which was disbanded on September 27, 1924. The Knights of Columbus organized the Nina Council in January 1887 under Grand Knight John D. Rooney. There were 30 members at its inception. In 1913, they purchased the Courtland Palmer House on Main Street to use as a meeting hall. In 1929, the group sold this home to the Holy Ghost Society. (Courtesy of the Stonington Historical Society.)

This 1975 photograph by Stonington photographer Rollie McKenna shows the annual Blessing of the Fleet. The event was revitalized in 2014 by St. Mary's Church. At center is a statue of St. Peter, which is traditionally placed on a float and brought from the church to the town dock. Another custom includes the awarding of a ceremonial wreath to the widow of the last fisherman lost at sea. The ceremony takes place every summer. (Courtesy of the Stonington Historical Society.)

In yet another Rollie McKenna photograph, spectators are enjoying complimentary Portuguese bread at the Portuguese Holy Ghost Society of Stonington's annual Feast of the Holy Ghost. The festivities usually take place every August and include music, traditional Portuguese cuisine, auctions, a blessing of seven lucky homes, and the selection of the coming year's feast sponsor. (Courtesy of the Stonington Historical Society.)

This photograph shows a meeting of the Thomas Stanton Society in Stonington. The society honors the life and work of Thomas Stanton, founder of Hartford and Stonington. (Courtesy of Nancy Ryan.)

This 1975 Rollie McKenna photograph shows Manuel Sardo (center) in front of the Portuguese Holy Ghost Society at 26 Main Street. The crowds are gathered to celebrate auction day during the annual Feast of the Holy Ghost. Auctioned items typically include Portuguese Azorean traditional specialties like sweetbread and seafood, which were eaten by Portuguese sailors who manned most of the whaling fleets in the mid-19th century, around the time of the origin of the feast in Connecticut. (Courtesy of Stonington Historical Society.)

Pictured here in a Rollie McKenna photograph during the Stonington Portuguese Holy Ghost Club's annual Feast of the Holy Ghost are, from left to right, Anna Pinheiro "Pine" Buridck, Bridgette Travers, Anna Travers, and Della Grieser. The festival is a relic from Portugal in the Middle Ages, brought to the Azores by settlers. Whalers then carried the tradition with them to Colonial America in the 1800s. The festival is still celebrated in Portugal, the Azores, and in most Portuguese communities, including Stonington. (Courtesy of Stonington Historical Society.)

The Wadawanuck Club is photographed here by Rollie McKenna. From left to right are sailing instructor Al Daggett, Nancy Gibson, Ken Tate, Dick Woolworth, and Rodney Johnstone. Originally established in 1908, the private club still offers summer activities such as sailing, swimming, and tennis, and has hosted Special Olympics sailing regattas. The current clubhouse on Water Street was constructed after the club's facilities were destroyed in the hurricane of 1938. (Courtesy of Stonington Historical Society.)

Rollie McKenna captured these spectators at a tennis match at the Wadawanuck Club. During the summer, the club hosts tennis matches, sailing regattas, charity events, weddings, and other events. (Courtesy of Stonington Historical Society.)

Amateur photographers are seen here on the "Picture Train" on June 22, 1937. The New Haven Railroad train ran from New York City to Stonington, where the camera enthusiasts could spend the day taking photos in the picturesque town and surrounding countryside. (Collection of M. Earl Smith.)

Another photograph from June 22, 1937, shows photographers from the Picture Train strolling through Stonington. According to the caption, "the young lady on the left evidently anticipated their arrival." (Collection of M. Earl Smith.)

This photograph, taken on May 25, 1969, by an AP photographer, shows a mother swan and six cygnets on a pond in Stonington. There is a Swan Street in Stonington, a historical Swan family who has roots in the area, and a rental home called the Black Swan. (Collection of M. Earl Smith.)

A group of children are playing marbles on School Street, facing Trumball Street. (Courtesy of the Stonington Historical Society.)

Shown here preparing to celebrate an event in Stonington are several citizens and a dog in Cannon Square. In spite of the fact that an accidental cannon discharge killed Thomas Stanton in 1815, the cannon has always been a patriotic emblem of the town. In 1913, the Battle of Stonington centennial adopted an emblem that pictured these two cannons and the memorial monument in the square. (Courtesy of the Stonington Historical Society.)

On September 21, 1938, the strongest hurricane in the history of New England made landfall on Long Island and moved up the coast, leaving destruction and mayhem in its wake. Stonington, was not excluded. Shown here is West Church Street shortly after the hurricane. At far right is 98 Water Street, which still stands today fully restored. The storm surge was so powerful that it swept some homes off their foundations and pushed them three miles inland. (Courtesy of the Stonington Historical Society.)

Shown here at the corner of Elm and Cliff Streets is one of the many fire brigades that took part in the Fireman's Parade during the centennial celebration of the Battle of Stonington on August 8–10, 1914. Among the brigades represented were Stonington Fire Engine Company No. 1; chiefs from Mystic, New London, and Noank; Pioneer Hook & Ladder Company No. 1, Stonington Fire Police, Mystic Hook & Ladder No. 1; and the B.F. Hoxie Engine Company No. 1. The parade took place on Saturday at 2:00 p.m. (Courtesy of the Stonington Historical Society.)

Children are pictured on the Fourth of July in 1881. In the background hangs a banner with a Confederate flag. This photograph was taken in the basement of the old Road Church, which had been rebuilt in 1829 and was serving as the town hall for the borough. (Courtesy of the Stonington Historical Society.)

Children skate on Elihu's Pond, with the American Velvet Company mill looming in the background. The pond came to be used for sport after the marsh on Cutler Street was drained. Gypsy moths laid eggs in the bushes surrounding the pond, leading to an effort by the state to eradicate their nesting grounds. The American Velvet Company mill has been repurposed into the Velvet Mill, which hosts fine art gatherings, eateries, and the Stonington Farmers Market. (Courtesy of the Stonington Historical Society.)

This stone bridge led to the wooden gazebo in the center of Walnut Grove in Stonington. The grove and the pond were documented at least twice by the state, in 1908 and 1910. Walnut Grove has also been called the Day Place, and at one time was part of the estate of Gershom Lambert. The site passed through several owners before becoming the home of the Stonington Manor Inn. (Courtesy of the Stonington Historical Society.)

The Second Congregational Church was formed in 1834 and lasted until it merged with the First Baptist Church in 1950 to become the United Church of Stonington. On November 11, 1833, John C. Nichols was named the first pastor, a role he filled until 1839. On April 12, 1834, the first building for the church was dedicated. On April 7, 1839, Rev. Jonathan E. Edwards was named the second pastor, serving until 1843, followed by Rev. William Clift. (Collection of M. Earl Smith.)

The Wadawanuck Club is on Water Street across from the viaduct at the headwaters of Stonington Harbor. The founding members were Edward F. Darrell, Charles H. Simmons, J. Culbert Palmer, and Judge Gilbert C. Collins. The facilities started as a private tennis club in 1908 and soon expanded to a private beach, boathouse, and other amenities. The present clubhouse was built and opened in 1940. (Collection of M. Earl Smith.)

This antique dollhouse was on display at the Lighthouse Museum at 7 Water Street. This photograph was taken by B.L. Gordon for a postcard published by the Book & Tackle Shop. (Collection of M. Earl Smith.)

On June 6, 1905, St. Mary's Church hosted a charity ball. On May 26, 1909, a drama club was organized by the parishioners. The church was home to weddings, such as the union between Katherine Smith and George Francis on October 26, 1910. The only citizen of Stonington who died in World War I, James W. Harvey, was buried with military honors in St. Mary's Cemetery on March 22, 1921. In February 1936, a Boy Scout troop was formed at St Mary's. (Collection of M. Earl Smith.)

On October 5, 1851, St. Mary's was dedicated. Bishop O' Reilly was in charge of the dedication. The church had three leaders in its first three years, as Catholicism sought to gain a foothold in the largely Protestant southeastern Connecticut. The fourth leadership change came in 1857. Another change followed in 1859. In 1861, St. Michael's was built, and St. Mary's became an out-mission to the new church. In 1871, St. Mary's came under the responsibility of St. Patrick's in Mystic. St. Mary's regained its parish status in 1901. (Collection of M. Earl Smith.)

When Rev. James Noyes arrived in Stonington in 1664, he had little idea that he would stay for 10 years, much less start what is now considered the oldest church in Stonington. After tense debate, the current site of the Road Church was agreed upon on September 14, 1671, on what was thereafter called "Agreement Hill." The church came to life on June 3, 1674, with nine members at its founding, including members of the Stanton, Chesebrough, Miner, Palmer, and Wheeler families. (Collection of M. Earl Smith.)

This photograph shows the end of Water Street, which leads past the lighthouse and out to Stonington Point. In 1924, the borough proposed a plan to remove many trees from the sides of the street to facilitate paving, but the New London County Commissioners ruled that the trees had to remain. On March 20, 1931, the borough voted to install streetlights on Water Street, from High Street to Diving Street. The great hurricane of 1938 stacked debris 15 feet high on Water Street. (Collection of M. Earl Smith.)

Five

THE CHOSEN ONE(S)

THE PEOPLE OF STONINGTON

Prominent Stonington politician Gilbert Collins served as the state representative for the area. Collins was born on April 14, 1790, and began life as a farmer. He married three times, to Prudence Frink, Lucy Breed, and Susan Wells. Prudence bore him three children (Benjamin Franklin, Anne, and Daniel), and Lucy bore him Gilbert, Ethan, and John. He died shortly before the end of the Civil War, on March 24, 1865. (Courtesy of the Library of Congress.)

This banner on Water Street, looking north from Pearl Street, shows support for Supreme Court justice Charles Evan Hughes in his unsuccessful bid to unseat Woodrow Wilson in the 1916 presidential election. Hughes, a Republican, won Connecticut by 6,728 votes but lost to Wilson by nearly 600,000 votes. (Courtesy of the Stonington Historical Society.)

Stonington Cemetery at 345 North Main Street has in the past also been known as Evergreen Cemetery. It opened in 1754 as the family cemetery of the Cheesebroughs. In addition to the remains of its founders, it holds the graves of poet James Merrill, writer Stephen Vincent Benet, poet J.D. McClatchy, artist Patti Hill, explorer Nathaniel Palmer, and others, including the two pictured above. (Collection of M. Earl Smith.)

This horse-drawn hearse sits outside the Robinson Burial Ground, founded in 1771 by English captain Thomas Robinson. Ironically, Robinson purchased the land on what is now known as Stonington Point from the Cheesebrough family, who had opened a cemetery in Stonington in 1754. During the War of 1812, a British bombshell landed on the property, which allowed Hulda Hall a convenient hole for burying her recently departed mother, Elisabeth. Hulda was buried next to her in 1830, although it would be 1900 before she was honored by the Children of the Revolution with a marker. (Courtesy of the Stonington Historical Society.)

Situated in the Wequetequock Cemetery are the remains of Stonington cofounder Thomas Stanton and his wife, Anna Lord. Stanton was born in England sometime around 1616 and first appears in the historical record as an interpreter for John Winthrop Jr., one of Connecticut's earliest governors. After nearly dying in the Pequot War, he served as a delegate to peace negotiations in 1638. He was appointed Indian interpreter for the United Colonies of New England in 1643. Around 1650, Stanton received permission to set up a settlement in what is now Stonington, which included a three-year monopoly on Indian trade in the area. (Courtesy of Nancy Ryan.)

Frank G. Sylvia was a businessman and farmer of Stonington known for owning a piece of land that contained one of the few prerevolutionary gristmills in the borough. Known as Fellows' Mill, it was erected on Stony Brook. It was first owned by Dr. William Lord, then Capt. Charles H. Smith, who erected a new dam to replace the old mill. Ownership passed to Sylvia in 1863. In 1865, he signed a 99-year lease with the New York, Providence & Boston Railroad Company, which used the pond to supply water to its locomotives and steamers. The pond later became part of the Greenwich Water Company in 1977. (Courtesy of the Stonington Historical Society.)

Shown here standing in front of the former Stonington Borough Hall at 18 Grand Street is Cornelius Crandall. In 1913, Crandall was appointed to the Stonington Battle Centennial Committee, which was given $3,000 to plan a memorial for the Battle of Stonington during the War of 1812. In his duties as warden, Crandall planted a tree for the centennial in Wadawanuck Park. On October 20, he accepted two Portuguese flags on behalf of the borough in honor of the Portuguese residents of the area. He died on February 9, 1933, after 37 years of service to Stonington. (Courtesy of the Stonington Historical Society.)

Raoul M. Delagrange wore many hats in his years in Stonington. He served in the Pioneer Hook & Ladder Company. In 1909, he purchased the marine and engine supply shop pictured here and added a machine shop. On March 11, 1917, he was named to the reorganized Stonington Board of Trade. In 1920, he built "the most up to date garage in 100 miles." On July 6, 1925, he was named chief engineer of the Stonington Fire District. He passed away in 1954. (Courtesy of the Stonington Historical Society.)

Shown here in front of their house at 134 Water Street is Paul and Katherine (Squadrito) Schepis. The pair were married on August 29, 1915, and a reception followed at her parents' house. On May 30, 1925, Paul opened a new store on Water Street, which served as an ice cream parlor, a deli, and a fruit and groceries store. Katherine died in 1965, and Paul in 1983. Their house is now the home of Indigo Blue, a women's designer boutique. (Courtesy of the Stonington Historical Society.)

Shown at right is iconic businessman William Park Bindloss, born on January 10, 1854, in Stonington. In 1893, he took partial ownership in a coal delivery service. He took full ownership in 1897. The same year, he cofounded the Exile Checker Club. Later that year, he served as worthy patron for Stonington's Order of the Eastern Star. In 1909, he invented an underwater boat exhaust. The next year, he organized the West Mystic Motor Boat Company. His daughter Ruth married in 1919. In 1920, he was elected borough burgess. He died on December 27, 1940. (Courtesy of the Stonington Historical Society.)

Shown at his desk is First Selectman Rob Simmons, who served Stonington and the entire Second Congressional District in Congress from 2001 to 2007. A retired US Army colonel, Simmons is also a former chair of the Yankee Institute for Public Policy in Hartford, a conservative think tank. He served during the Vietnam war. (Collection of M. Earl Smith.)

Pictured here is early Hollywood star Dorothy Comingore. Although she was first discovered by Charlie Chaplin, much of her career was self-made. Cast as Susan Alexander in the 1941 masterpiece *Citizen Kane*, she gained rave reviews from both critics and the public. Unfortunately, the film, based loosely on media tycoon William Randolph Hearst, would be her downfall, as Hearst used his influence to have her put on an FBI watchlist for "distributing Communist literature to Negroes." She refused to testify before the House Committee on Un-American Activities. In retaliation, she lost custody of her children and was falsely arrested for prostitution. She later moved to Stonington, where, in 1971, she died of a respiratory infection. (Collection of M. Earl Smith.)

Shown here performing in *The Secret of Santa Vittoria* is Italian-American singer and actor Sergio Franchi. Although he originally trained as a classical opera singer, Franchi focused more on mainstream American pop music. He performed at the MGM Grand for several years starting in the 1970s. In 1979, after much success in both music and film, he purchased a 240-acre estate in Stonington. The estate is now located on Sergio Franchi Drive. Franchi died of a brain tumor at his Stonington estate on May 1, 1990. His estate hosted a memorial concert until 2019, with proceeds going to a scholarship fund named after the artist. (Collection of M. Earl Smith.)

Shown here is the headstone of Capt. John Stanton, one of at least 10 children of town founder Thomas Stanton. Captain Stanton was born in Hartford in 1641 and was elected town clerk in 1664. After studying at Harvard, he was commissioned a captain in the British army, serving as one of four captains during King Philip's War. He was reelected town clerk in 1674 and held that office until 1699. He sold 200 acres to Isaac Wheeler in 1687, which became the Wheeler farm. Stanton passed away in 1713, on Halloween. (Courtesy of Robert Stanton.)

Shown here in front of the family home on Elm Street is Helen Mae Koelb. This photograph was taken sometime between 1910 and 1920, as Helen and her family had relocated to Westerly Road by the 1920 Census. Thus, she was between 15 and 25 at the time of this photograph. Her father, Carl Koelb, was the head of the Rossie Velvet Mill. Helen's mother was Carrie, and she had three younger brothers: Ralph and twins Howard and Milton. The 1930 Census lists Helen's status as an "inmate" at Norwich State Hospital. She died in 1931, at the age of 36, during a tuberculosis outbreak. She is buried in Evergreen Cemetery. (Collection of M. Earl Smith.)

Shown here is the headstone of Thomas Lord, who could be considered one of the "grandfathers" of Stonington. Born in 1585, Lord was one of those responsible for the settlement of Hartford. His daughter Anna married Thomas Stanton, one of the four founding fathers of Stonington, in 1637. The pair moved to Stonington sometime around 1658, and Stanton was named deputy in 1666. Thomas Lord died in 1678 at the age of 93. His remains are interred in Hartford's Ancient Burying Ground, beneath this brown headstone. (Courtesy of Nancy Ryan.)

Once the owner of the famous Amos Palmer House, author Stephen Vincent Benet was one of many literary transplants to Stonington. A graduate of Yale University, Benet was a poet, a short story writer, and a novelist. His many and numerous awards include two Pulitzer Prizes for poetry and an O. Henry Award. He received a Guggenheim Fellowship, was elected to the American Academy of Arts and Letters in 1929, and was named a fellow of the American Academy of Arts and Sciences in 1931. Sadly, he died prematurely at the age of 44 of a heart attack. He is buried in Evergreen Cemetery. (Collection of M. Earl Smith.)

In addition to the ties that Steven Spielberg has to Stonington thanks to his film *Amistad*, the director has an earlier connection to the area. His 1975 film *Jaws* is based on the 1974 book that was written, in part, in a converted chicken coop at the old Wesson farm in Stonington. Author Peter Benchley, pictured here, wrote the book at a time in his life when he felt he needed to give writing one last chance. Benchley was also a speechwriter for Lyndon B. Johnson and a reporter for the *Washington Post* and *Newsweek*. His son Clayton was born in Stonington in 1969. (Collection of M. Earl Smith.)

Award-winning essayist Eleanor Perenyi was one of many influential literary voices to inhabit Stonington at one time or another. She was the daughter of Navy officer Ellis S. Stone and author Grace Zaring Stone, who wrote her anti-Nazi novel *Escape* under the pseudonym of Ethel Vance to protect her daughter, who was living in fascist-led Hungary at the time. Perenyi's best-known work is *Green Thoughts*, a collection of essays based on her gardening experiences in Ukraine. She won an award in literature from the American Academy of Arts and Letters in 1982. She passed away in Stonington in 2009. (Collection of M. Earl Smith.)

Actress Ruth Buzzi's family migrated from Italian-speaking portions of Switzerland to settle in Stonington. Born in 1936, she is the daughter of Rena and Angelo Buzzi. The family has owned Buzzi Memorials in Stonington since 1933. Ruth is a graduate of Stonington High School. Her accomplishments in the world of stage and screen are far too numerous to list here but include Emmy nominations, a Golden Globe award, and an NAACP Image Award, as well as appearances in over 20 films and TV shows such as *CHIPs*, *Days of Our Lives*, *The Love Boat*, and *Saved by the Bell*. (Collection of M. Earl Smith.)

One of Stonington's more colorful current residents is the soft-spoken Greg "Fossilman" Raymer, who purchased property in the area after winning the 2004 World Series of Poker main event. Before becoming a world champion poker player, Raymer was a patent attorney for Pfizer, which has a research facility in nearby Groton. Raymer was held at gunpoint by two men who sought to rob him of his winnings in 2004, but was able to hold them off until police arrived. (Collection of M. Earl Smith.)

This photograph shows a baseball club in Stonington around 1920. In 1855, nine players formed the Wadawanuck Baseball Club. In 1874, the borough organized the Lively Fleas baseball club. In 1886, the first black team was formed. In 1901, a club called Fisherman & Farmers was organized. Two people born in Stonington made it to the major leagues: Wally Kopf, who played two games for the New York Giants in 1922, and Matty McIntyre, who played 11 seasons (1901–1912) for the Athletics, Tigers, and White Sox. (Courtesy of the Stonington Historical Society.)

The first reunion of the Palmer family was hosted in 1881, and it had everything—hundreds of people, the band pictured here, and even a song sung outside the reunion tent by some ruffian who no doubt did not match the quality of music offered by the band. His lyrics, according to the *Norwich News*, included, "Bring the psalter, I sing of Walter; I'm a psalmer, my name is Palmer / Great man I am, You-be-dam. / There were Palmers on land and Palmers on sea / And Palmers from jail where most ought to be." (Courtesy of the Stonington Historical Society.)

Shown here sitting in a chair with two broken ankles is pharmacist Charles T. Willard, born January 29, 1864, in New York City. His first moment of note in Stonington was on June 19, 1891, when he and Richard F. Loper won the Wadawanuck Tennis Club's doubles championship. In 1901, it was said his boat *Squid* was the fastest in Stonington Harbor. He placed it up for sale in April 1905. In 1906, he joined the New Jersey Pharmaceutical Association. In 1908, he and C.P. Williams took a car trip to New York City. He sold his pharmacy and retired in 1923. He died in 1939 in Stonington and is buried in New Jersey. (Courtesy of the Stonington Historical Society.)

Shown here holding a copy of the score to the operetta *Katinka* is Merton Perry Clark of Stonington. The husband of Helen M. (Hobart) Clark, Merton was born in Stonington on June 25, 1892, and graduated from Stonington High School and the New London College of Business. He spent 30 years as an accountant at H.A. Austin before retiring and working part-time at the New England Science Center. He volunteered his time in the book department at the Salvation Army until he was 90. He was known as an accomplished violinist, pianist, and organist and once conducted his own orchestra. He died on August 2, 1991, at the age of 99 and is buried in Mystic. (Collection of M. Earl Smith.)

Rev. Dr. Albert Gallatin Palmer, a direct descendant of Walter Palmer, is pictured here. Palmer was born in Stonington in 1813 and became a prolific Baptist preacher whose sermons were heard in New York, Rhode Island, Massachusetts, and Stonington between the 1830s and 1890s. He published multiple religious hymn texts and contributed to Stonington community events like the dry centennial celebration of the Battle of Stonington. (Courtesy of the Stonington Historical Society.)

Capt. Alexander Smith Palmer, another descendant of Stonington founder Walter Palmer, was born in Stonington in 1806 and became known for his sea voyages. He began as a boy of 15, and at the age of 21 found himself on the *Penguin* on Antarctic sealing expeditions with his brother Capt. Nathaniel Palmer. At the age of 25, Alexander S. Palmer became the commander of the *Charles Adams* and continued his career until the age of 42. He went on to serve as Connecticut state representative three times and as state senator twice. (Courtesy of the Stonington Historical Society.)

Albert Sherr and his new bride, Elizabeth Babcock (the great-granddaughter of Alexander Palmer), are pictured on the east side of the Palmer House in front of its original cast-iron fence in October 1949. Scherr was the son of the vice president of the Dime Savings Bank of New York and was a prolific engineer who held several patents for electronics production. (Courtesy of the Stonington Historical Society.)

Prolific businessman Eugene Atwood is pictured in this turn-of-the-20th-century photograph. Atwood was the president of the Atwood Machine Company, which was relocated to Stonington in 1876 by his father, John Edwin Atwood, after the original location in Willimantic burned down. The company prospered selling silk machines out of the Trumbull factory for 70 years. In 1916, Atwood established a trust fund to benefit hardworking, ambitious teens. The Eugene Atwood Fund still exists, and two of Atwood's great-grandchildren and two of his great-great-grandchildren serve as trustees. (Courtesy of Stonington Historical Society.)

A group of men are pictured aboard a fishing boat in Stonington Harbor. Immigrants from Asia have a long history in the fishing industry in the United States. The presence of a commercial fishing fleet has attracted expert fishermen to Connecticut for over a century. (Courtesy of the Stonington Historical Society.)

Shown here enjoying a fun day in the sun on one of Stonington's many ferries is Eliza Niles (Trumbull) Robinson, with her back to the camera. The daughter of Stonington legend John F. Trumbull, she was born in 1839. In 1862, she married Henry C. Robinson, a prominent Republican and lawyer who would stand for the office of governor twice and served two terms as the mayor of Hartford. The two had five children: Lucius F., Lucy T., Henry S., John T., and Mary S. (Courtesy of Stonington Historical Society.)

The Stonington-born seal hunter and explorer Capt. Nathaniel B. Palmer (1799–1877) was a direct descendant of Stonington founder Walter Palmer. Capt. Nathaniel Palmer is well-known for guiding the first group of American sailors to reach the Antarctic peninsula in 1820, a part of which was named Palmer Land. Palmer became a sea captain at the age of 21. Not long after, in the mid-1800s, he became a ship designer, employing his years of expertise in developing improvements to various ships. (Courtesy of Stonington Historical Society.)

Eliza T. Babcock married Capt. Nathaniel Palmer in December 1826 when she was 16 years old and he was 27. The two could never bear children; however, this gave Eliza the opportunity to voyage with her husband. On one particularly harrowing journey to the Juan Fernandez archipelago off South America, their ship was commandeered by over 100 convicts, and she was locked in a room with bread and water. Captain Palmer was forced to deliver the criminals to the mainland, but both he and his wife survived. (Courtesy Stonington Historical Society.)

William Park Bindloss was a coal merchant from Stonington. Born in neighboring Groton in 1854, he was educated at Mystic High School and began working on a local farm at age 14. He then went on to practice masonry for 15 years. He married Elizabeth Esther Bickley in 1881 and built a house on Water Street in 1884. They had two children before he entered into the lucrative coal business, for which he is best known, at the age of 43. (Courtesy of Stonington Historical Society.)

Zebulon Hancox is seen here at the turn of the 20th century. Rumor has it that Hancox spent his adult life as a miser while laboring to build a fortune on real estate and fishing—all to win the heart of a young woman who had rejected him in youth due to his poverty. Some of the homes he built in the mid- to late 1800s still stand on Hancox Street (named after him), including the historic Rose Cottage. He died single at 91 with a fortune to his name. (Courtesy of Stonington Historical Society.)

Camelo La Grua poses outside of his shoe repair business at 111 Water Street. La Grua was an Italian immigrant whose son Maurice went on to earn two Purple Hearts in World War II before returning to Stonington to become a professional photographer. Maurice later opened a gift shop just down the street from his father's business. After Maurice's passing in 2005, his wife, Winifred, started a foundation in their names to revitalize the old foundry as the La Grua Center, which opened its doors in 2008 and holds classes and events seven days a week. (Courtesy of Stonington Historical Society.)

Vivien Kellems, seen here in 1956, was president (and part-owner, with her brother) of the Kellems Company, founded in 1937 in Stonington. She became famous when she refused to collect withholding taxes from her employees. Kellems was also a fervent supporter of both voting reform and the Equal Rights Amendment. (Collection of M. Earl Smith.)

Shown here behind the bar at the Sea Village Apartments (formerly the Sea View Restaurant and Bar) is Carl Rosen. In addition to his occasional stints behind the bar, Rosen was the foreman of Steamer Engine No. 1, a position where he presented a badge to comedian and radio personality Ed Wynn in June 1935. The Perrys opened the restaurant in 1938, only to see it immediately destroyed by the great hurricane of 1938. They rebuilt and reopened in 1939. The establishment was used in 1946 to honor pharmacist Francis J. Connors. (Courtesy of the Stonington Historical Society.)

Mary Howe, who would become affectionately known as "Aunt Mary Howe," inhabited what was originally known as the Thomas Howe House, on the corner of Main and Church Streets. In 1887, she rented the home to the newly formed Stonington Library Association for $100 a year; the building served as Stonington's library until 1899. Howe also played a key role in organizing the first Sunday school services for the First Congregational Church. She was born on August 21, 1804, and passed away on May 23, 1887. She is buried in Evergreen Cemetery. (Courtesy of the Stonington Historical Society.)

Shown here with patriotic decor covering their storefront on Hancock Street are Joseph M. and Mary Perry. Joseph was born in 1888 and died in 1947. He had a hand in the purchase of the house on Main Street that once belonged to the Knights of Columbus for the Holy Ghost Society, in January 1929, and was named the keeper of the estate. On August 6, 1938, he participated in burning the mortgage on the now paid property at a picnic in Waterford. Mary was born in 1896 and died in 1937. The third person is listed as Maurel Florence. (Courtesy of the Stonington Historical Society.)

Six

THAT'S A WEIRD ONE
THE QUIRKY SIDE OF STONINGTON

White Rock Dam straddled the line between Stonington and Westerly, Rhode Island. Built on the Pawcatuck River in 1940, the dam was eight miles from the mouth of the river. It was built to power the White Rock Mill, which was less than half a mile downstream from the dam itself. Funds were allocated in 2013 from Hurricane Sandy recovery money, and the dam was removed in 2016. (Collection of M. Earl Smith.)

Taken on Main Street just north of High Street, this photograph shows the beauty of Stonington in the winter. The area receives 27 inches of snow per year, on par with the national average of 28. (Courtesy of Stonington Historical Society.)

The boulders on Boulder Beach are a testament to geological activities that took place 500 million years ago. Around that time, much of what now constitutes the area was part of a continent now referred to as proto–North America, which was situated along the equator and surrounded by what is now called the Iapetus Ocean. Over the next 250 million years, it collided with other landmasses to form Pangea. Around 200 million years ago, the continents began drifting apart. The part of Connecticut that was on the North American plate was violently torn away from Africa, taking with it several large chunks of that continent. This action helped to form the Atlantic Ocean. (Both, courtesy of the Library of Congress.)

From a geological perspective, southeastern Connecticut, including Stonington, has more in common with Rhode Island, the Massachusetts cape, and the Maine shore than the rest of the state. This is due to the Avalonia terrane having been left behind when eastern North America and Africa separated. In fact, Stonington has more in common with the coast of northwest Africa than it does with the rest of North America. This includes large deposits of Westerly granite, some of which has been quarried. Three different terranes combined with North America to form Connecticut: Avalonia, Iapetus, and Newark, which forms the Hartford Valley. In the past 10 million years, several glaciers have covered Connecticut, North America, and Long Island Sound, including, most recently, the Wisconsin glacier. As these glaciers migrated across the landscape, they often pushed sediment across the surface, including rolling stones and rocking rocks, many of which dot the Stonington shoreline today. (Both, courtesy of the Library of Congress.)

This photograph, buried deep in the archives of the Stonington Historical Society, is labeled "Ruins of Sal Tinkins House." While little is known about the home itself, the house was most likely destroyed by the 1938 hurricane. This hurricane caused $306 million in property damage (roughly $4.7 billion in 2020) and left effects that were still showing as late as 1951. The storm had winds that exceeded 160 miles per hour. In Mystic, crabs and live fish were found in cabinets and drawers of homes. The storm claimed the lives of 682 people. (Courtesy of the Stonington Historical Society.)

DISCOVER THOUSANDS OF LOCAL HISTORY BOOKS FEATURING MILLIONS OF VINTAGE IMAGES

Arcadia Publishing, the leading local history publisher in the United States, is committed to making history accessible and meaningful through publishing books that celebrate and preserve the heritage of America's people and places.

Find more books like this at
www.arcadiapublishing.com

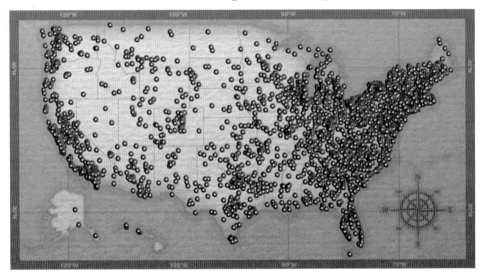

Search for your hometown history, your old stomping grounds, and even your favorite sports team.

Consistent with our mission to preserve history on a local level, this book was printed in South Carolina on American-made paper and manufactured entirely in the United States. Products carrying the accredited Forest Stewardship Council (FSC) label are printed on 100 percent FSC-certified paper.

MADE IN THE USA